Heavenly Realm Publishing
Houston, Texas

Copyright © 2017 Stephanie Franklin, The Biblical Bible Study Handbook: *The New Testament Study for the Individual and Small or Large Group Bible Study.* All rights reserved.

Published By:
Heavenly Realm Publishing
www.heavenlyrealmpublishing.com
Toll Free 1-866-216-0696

Printed in the United States of America

All rights reserved. No part of this book may be reproduced, stored in a retrieval system, or transmitted by any means, electronic, mechanical, photocopying, recording, or otherwise, without written permission from the author.

Scripture quotations are from the Holy Bible. All rights reserved.

ISBN—13: 978-1-944383-07-7 (paperback)

Library of Congress Cataloging-in-Publication Data: 2017911332
Stephanie Franklin
Biblical Bible Study Handbook: *The New Testament Study for the Individual and Small or Large Group Bible Study* / Stephanie Franklin

1. Religion: Biblical Reference - Handbooks—United States. **2.** Reference: Handbooks & Manuals—United States. **3.** Religion: Biblical Studies - Bible Study Guides—United States.

This book is printed on acid free paper.

Stephanie Franklin
Stephanie Franklin Ministries
www.stephaniefranklin.org
www.stephaniefranklinministries.org

The Biblical Bible Study Handbook

*The New Testament Study for the Individual
and Small or Large Group Bible Study.*

The New Testament Study

*Study each chapter of the New Testament, write your notes,
and share and study with a small or large
Sunday School or Bible Study group.*

Stephanie Franklin

OTHER BOOKS BY STEPHANIE

FICTION NOVELS & MOTIVATIONAL BOOKS:

1. When Ramona Got Her Groove Back from God
2. My Song of Solomon
3. My Song of Solomon *Prayer Journal*
4. God Loves Thugs Too!
5. The Locker Room Experience: *For the Struggling Athlete & Coach, & Tips on How to Get Recruited in Sports*
6. RE*shape* YOU: *A Fitness Guide to Teach You How to Create the NEW YOU from the Inside Out*
7. RE*shape* YOU Elderly Fitness Exercises & Eating Plan Book
8. The Peacemaker: *Avoiding & Resolving Conflicts Within Relationships, the Church & in the Work Place*
9. DO IT ON PURPOSE: *How to Respond When Challenges Try to Pull You Away from God's Purpose for Your Life*

MINISTRY BOOKS & WORKBOOK:

10. Position Your Faith for Great Success
11. Position Your Faith for Great Success *Workbook*
12. The Purpose Chaser: *For Children Ages 5 to 12*
13. Church Hurt: *How to Heal & Overcome It*
14. The Power of Healing
15. The Power of the Holy Spirit
16. Winning Together: *His Needs Matter, Her Needs Are Important*
17. Winning Together as a Parent: *Loving Each Other While Knowing Your Children and Teen are Included and Not Separate.*
18. The Biblical Bible Study Handbook: *The Old Testament Study for the Individual and Small or Large Group Bible Study.*
19. The Biblical Bible Study Handbook: *The New Testament Study for the Individual and Small or Large Group Bible Study.*

Each book may be purchased at any Christian Bookstore, Barnes & Noble, Amazon.com, Books-a-Million, Borders, and anywhere books are sold.

The Books of the Bible

The New Testament

1.	Matthew	12	15.	1 Timothy	222
2.	Mark	34	16.	2 Timothy	234
3.	Luke	50	17.	Titus	244
4.	John	70	18.	Philemon	254
5.	Acts *(of the Apostles)*	90	19.	Hebrews	262
6.	Romans	112	20.	James	278
7.	1 Corinthians	128	21.	1 Peter	288
8.	2 Corinthians	144	22.	2 Peter	298
9.	Galatians	158	23.	1 John	308
10.	Ephesians	170	24.	2 John	320
11.	Philippians	182	25.	3 John	330
12.	Colossians	192	26.	Jude	338
13.	1 Thessalonians	202	27.	Revelation	346
14.	2 Thessalonians	212			

The Biblical Bible Study Handbook

Name of Individual Studying _____
Name of Group Studying *(a group is two or more people if applicable)*

1. _____
2. _____
3. _____
4. _____
5. _____
6. _____
7. _____
8. _____
9. _____
10. _____
11. _____
12. _____
13. _____
14. _____
15. _____
16. _____
17. _____
18. _____
19. _____
20. _____
21. _____
22. _____
23. _____
24. _____
25. _____
26. _____
27. _____
28. _____
29. _____
30. _____
31. _____

32. _____
33. _____
34. _____
35. _____
36. _____
37. _____
38. _____
39. _____
40. _____
41. _____
42. _____
43. _____
44. _____
45. _____
46. _____
47. _____
48. _____
49. _____
50. _____
51. _____
52. _____
53. _____
54. _____
55. _____
56. _____
57. _____
58. _____
59. _____
60. _____
61. _____
62. _____
63. _____
64. _____
65. _____
66. _____

67. _____
68. _____
69. _____
70. _____
71. _____
72. _____
73. _____
74. _____
75. _____
76. _____
77. _____
78. _____
79. _____
80. _____
81. _____
82. _____
83. _____
84. _____
85. _____
86. _____
87. _____
88. _____
89. _____
90. _____
91. _____
92. _____
93. _____
94. _____
95. _____
96. _____
97. _____
98. _____
99. _____
100. _____
101. _____

CHAPTER 1

The Book of Matthew

The Biblical Bible Study Handbook

TODAY'S DATE: _____

DATE BOOK WAS WRITTEN _____

NAME OF LESSON _____

BIBLICAL TEXT _____

SCRIPTURE(S):

_____

_____

_____

Who wrote this book?

_____

What is Chapter 1 about?

_____
_____
_____
_____
_____
_____
_____
_____
_____
_____
_____
_____
_____
_____
_____

What is Chapter 2 about?

_____

What is Chapter 3 about?

What is Chapter 4 about?

_____
_____
_____
_____
_____
_____
_____
_____
_____
_____
_____
_____
_____
_____
_____
_____
_____

What is Chapter 5 about?

_____
_____
_____
_____
_____
_____
_____
_____
_____
_____
_____
_____
_____
_____
_____
_____
_____

What is Chapter 6 about?

What is Chapter 7 about?

What is Chapter 8 about?

What is Chapter 9 about?

What is Chapter 10 about?

What is Chapter 11 about?

What is Chapter 12 about?

What is Chapter 13 about?

What is Chapter 14 about?

What is Chapter 15 about?

What is Chapter 16 about?

What is Chapter 17 about?

What is Chapter 18 about?

What is Chapter 19 about?
_____
_____
_____
_____
_____
_____
_____
_____
_____
_____
_____
_____
_____
_____
_____
_____

What is Chapter 20 about?
_____
_____
_____
_____
_____
_____
_____
_____
_____
_____
_____
_____
_____
_____
_____

What is Chapter 21 about?

What is Chapter 22 about?

What is Chapter 23 about?

What is Chapter 24 about?

What is Chapter 25 about?

What is Chapter 26 about?

What is Chapter 27 about?

What is Chapter 28 about?

What are some key verses that stand out to you?

Any words from God?

What revelation did you get from the text?

What is the entire book talking about?

POINTS FOR POWER: *(Write your points for Spiritual power through what the chapter is trying to convey that you will apply to your own life).*

1. _____

2.

3.

CHAPTER 2

The Book of Mark

TODAY'S DATE: _____
DATE BOOK WAS WRITTEN _____

NAME OF LESSON _____
BIBLICAL TEXT _____

SCRIPTURE(S):
_____
_____
_____

Who wrote this book?
_____

What is Chapter 1 about?
_____
_____
_____
_____
_____
_____
_____
_____
_____
_____
_____
_____
_____
_____
_____
_____

What is Chapter 2 about?
_____

What is Chapter 3 about?

What is Chapter 4 about?

What is Chapter 5 about?

What is Chapter 6 about?

What is Chapter 7 about?

What is Chapter 8 about?

What is Chapter 9 about?

What is Chapter 10 about?

What is Chapter 11 about?

What is Chapter 12 about?

What is Chapter 13 about?

What is Chapter 14 about?

What is Chapter 15 about?

What is Chapter 16 about?

What are some key verses that stand out to you?

Any words from God?

What revelation did you get from the text?

What is the entire book talking about?

POINTS FOR POWER: *(Write your points for Spiritual power through what the chapter is trying to convey that you will apply to your own life).*

1. _____

2.

3.

CHAPTER 3

The Book of Luke

TODAY'S DATE: _____

DATE BOOK WAS WRITTEN _____

NAME OF LESSON _____

BIBLICAL TEXT _____

SCRIPTURE(S):
_____
_____
_____

Who wrote this book?
_____

What is Chapter 1 about?
_____
_____
_____
_____
_____
_____
_____
_____
_____
_____
_____
_____
_____
_____
_____
_____

What is Chapter 2 about?
_____

What is Chapter 3 about?

What is Chapter 4 about?

What is Chapter 5 about?

What is Chapter 6 about?

What is Chapter 7 about?

What is Chapter 8 about?

What is Chapter 9 about?

What is Chapter 10 about?

What is Chapter 11 about?

What is Chapter 12 about?

What is Chapter 13 about?

What is Chapter 14 about?

What is Chapter 15 about?

What is Chapter 16 about?

What is Chapter 17 about?

What is Chapter 18 about?

What is Chapter 19 about?

What is Chapter 20 about?

What is Chapter 21 about?

What is Chapter 22 about?

What is Chapter 23 about?

What is Chapter 24 about?

What are some key verses that stand out to you?

Any words from God?

What revelation did you get from the text?

What is the entire book talking about?

POINTS FOR POWER: *(Write your points for Spiritual power through what the chapter is trying to convey that you will apply to your own life).*

1. _____

2.

3.

CHAPTER 4

The Book of John

TODAY'S DATE: _____

DATE BOOK WAS WRITTEN _____

NAME OF LESSON _____

BIBLICAL TEXT _____

SCRIPTURE(S):
_____
_____
_____

Who wrote this book?
_____

What is Chapter 1 about?
_____
_____
_____
_____
_____
_____
_____
_____
_____
_____
_____
_____
_____
_____
_____

What is Chapter 2 about?
_____

What is Chapter 3 about?

What is Chapter 4 about?

What is Chapter 5 about?

What is Chapter 6 about?

What is Chapter 7 about?

What is Chapter 8 about?

What is Chapter 9 about?

What is Chapter 10 about?

What is Chapter 11 about?

What is Chapter 12 about?

What is Chapter 13 about?

What is Chapter 14 about?

What is Chapter 15 about?

What is Chapter 16 about?

What is Chapter 17 about?

What is Chapter 18 about?

What is Chapter 19 about?

What is Chapter 20 about?

What is Chapter 21 about?

What are some key verses that stand out to you?

Any words from God?
_____
_____
_____
_____
_____
_____
_____
_____
_____
_____

What revelation did you get from the text?
_____
_____
_____
_____
_____
_____
_____
_____
_____
_____

What is the entire book talking about?
_____
_____
_____
_____
_____

POINTS FOR POWER: *(Write your points for Spiritual power through what the chapter is trying to convey that you will apply to your own life).*

1. _____

2. _____

3.

CHAPTER 5

The Book of Acts

TODAY'S DATE: _____
DATE BOOK WAS WRITTEN _____

NAME OF LESSON _____
BIBLICAL TEXT _____

SCRIPTURE(S):
_____
_____
_____

Who wrote this book?
_____

What is Chapter 1 about?
_____
_____
_____
_____
_____
_____
_____
_____
_____
_____
_____
_____
_____
_____
_____

What is Chapter 2 about?
_____

What is Chapter 3 about?

What is Chapter 4 about?

What is Chapter 5 about?

What is Chapter 6 about?

What is Chapter 7 about?

What is Chapter 8 about?

What is Chapter 9 about?

What is Chapter 10 about?

What is Chapter 11 about?

What is Chapter 12 about?

What is Chapter 13 about?

What is Chapter 14 about?

What is Chapter 15 about?

What is Chapter 16 about?

What is Chapter 17 about?

What is Chapter 18 about?

What is Chapter 19 about?

What is Chapter 20 about?

What is Chapter 21 about?

What is Chapter 22 about?

What is Chapter 23 about?

What is Chapter 24 about?

What is Chapter 25 about?

What is Chapter 26 about?

What is Chapter 27 about?

What is Chapter 28 about?

What are some key verses that stand out to you?

Any words from God?

What revelation did you get from the text?

What is the entire book talking about?

POINTS FOR POWER: *(Write your points for Spiritual power through what the chapter is trying to convey that you will apply to your own life).*

1. _____

2.

3.

CHAPTER 6

The Book of Romans

TODAY'S DATE: _____

DATE BOOK WAS WRITTEN _____

NAME OF LESSON _____

BIBLICAL TEXT _____

SCRIPTURE(S):
_____
_____
_____

Who wrote this book?
_____

What is Chapter 1 about?
_____
_____
_____
_____
_____
_____
_____
_____
_____
_____
_____
_____
_____
_____
_____
_____

What is Chapter 2 about?
_____

What is Chapter 3 about?

What is Chapter 4 about?

What is Chapter 5 about?

What is Chapter 6 about?

What is Chapter 7 about?

What is Chapter 8 about?

What is Chapter 9 about?

What is Chapter 10 about?

What is Chapter 11 about?

What is Chapter 12 about?

What is Chapter 13 about?

What is Chapter 14 about?

What is Chapter 15 about?

What is Chapter 16 about?

What are some key verses that stand out to you?

Any words from God?

What revelation did you get from the text?

What is the entire book talking about?

POINTS FOR POWER: *(Write your points for Spiritual power through what the chapter is trying to convey that you will apply to your own life).*

1. _____

2.

3.

CHAPTER 7

The Book of 1 Corinthians

TODAY'S DATE: _____

DATE BOOK WAS WRITTEN _____

NAME OF LESSON _____

BIBLICAL TEXT _____

SCRIPTURE(S):

_____

_____

_____

Who wrote this book?

_____

What is Chapter 1 about?

_____

_____

_____

_____

_____

_____

_____

_____

_____

_____

_____

_____

_____

_____

What is Chapter 2 about?

_____

What is Chapter 3 about?

What is Chapter 4 about?

What is Chapter 5 about?

What is Chapter 6 about?

What is Chapter 7 about?

What is Chapter 8 about?

What is Chapter 9 about?

What is Chapter 10 about?

What is Chapter 11 about?

What is Chapter 12 about?

What is Chapter 13 about?

What is Chapter 14 about?

What is Chapter 15 about?

What is Chapter 16 about?

What are some key verses that stand out to you?

Any words from God?

What revelation did you get from the text?

What is the entire book talking about?

POINTS FOR POWER: *(Write your points for Spiritual power through what the chapter is trying to convey that you will apply to your own life).*

1. _____

2.

3.

CHAPTER 8

The Book of 2 Corinthians

TODAY'S DATE: _____
DATE BOOK WAS WRITTEN _____

NAME OF LESSON _____
BIBLICAL TEXT _____

SCRIPTURE(S):
_____
_____
_____

Who wrote this book?
_____

What is Chapter 1 about?
_____
_____
_____
_____
_____
_____
_____
_____
_____
_____
_____
_____
_____
_____
_____

What is Chapter 2 about?
_____

What is Chapter 3 about?

What is Chapter 4 about?

What is Chapter 5 about?

What is Chapter 6 about?

What is Chapter 7 about?

What is Chapter 8 about?

What is Chapter 9 about?

What is Chapter 10 about?

What is Chapter 11 about?

What is Chapter 12 about?

What is Chapter 13 about?

What are some key verses that stand out to you?

Any words from God?

What revelation did you get from the text?

What is the entire book talking about?

POINTS FOR POWER: *(Write your points for Spiritual power through what the chapter is trying to convey that you will apply to your own life).*

1. _____
_____
_____

2.

3.

CHAPTER 9

The Book of Galatians

TODAY'S DATE: _____
DATE BOOK WAS WRITTEN _____

NAME OF LESSON _____
BIBLICAL TEXT _____

SCRIPTURE(S):
_____
_____
_____

Who wrote this book?
_____

What is Chapter 1 about?
_____
_____
_____
_____
_____
_____
_____
_____
_____
_____
_____
_____
_____
_____
_____
_____
_____

What is Chapter 2 about?
_____

What is Chapter 3 about?

What is Chapter 4 about?

What is Chapter 5 about?

What is Chapter 6 about?

What are some key verses that stand out to you?

Any words from God?

_____
_____
_____
_____
_____
_____
_____
_____
_____
_____

What revelation did you get from the text?

_____
_____
_____
_____
_____
_____
_____
_____
_____
_____

What is the entire book talking about?

_____
_____
_____
_____
_____

POINTS FOR POWER: *(Write your points for Spiritual power through what the chapter is trying to convey that you will apply to your own life).*

1. _____

2.

3.

CHAPTER 10

The Book of Ephesians

TODAY'S DATE: _____

DATE BOOK WAS WRITTEN _____

NAME OF LESSON _____

BIBLICAL TEXT _____

SCRIPTURE(S):

_____

_____

_____

Who wrote this book?

_____

What is Chapter 1 about?

_____
_____
_____
_____
_____
_____
_____
_____
_____
_____
_____
_____
_____
_____
_____
_____

What is Chapter 2 about?

_____

What is Chapter 3 about?

What is Chapter 4 about?

What is Chapter 5 about?

What is Chapter 6 about?

What are some key verses that stand out to you?

Any words from God?

_____
_____
_____
_____
_____
_____
_____
_____
_____
_____

What revelation did you get from the text?

_____
_____
_____
_____
_____
_____
_____
_____
_____
_____

What is the entire book talking about?

_____
_____
_____
_____
_____

The Biblical Bible Study Handbook

POINTS FOR POWER: *(Write your points for Spiritual power through what the chapter is trying to convey that you will apply to your own life).*

1.

2.

3.

CHAPTER 11

The Book of Philippians

TODAY'S DATE: _____
DATE BOOK WAS WRITTEN _____

NAME OF LESSON _____
BIBLICAL TEXT _____

SCRIPTURE(S):
_____
_____
_____

Who wrote this book?
_____

What is Chapter 1 about?
_____
_____
_____
_____
_____
_____
_____
_____
_____
_____
_____
_____
_____
_____
_____

What is Chapter 2 about?
_____

What is Chapter 3 about?

What is Chapter 4 about?

_____
_____
_____
_____
_____
_____
_____
_____
_____
_____
_____
_____
_____
_____
_____
_____
_____

What are some key verses that stand out to you?

_____
_____
_____
_____
_____
_____
_____
_____
_____
_____
_____

Any words from God?

_____

What revelation did you get from the text?

What is the entire book talking about?

POINTS FOR POWER: *(Write your points for Spiritual power through what the chapter is trying to convey that you will apply to your own life).*

1. _____

2.

3.

CHAPTER 12

The Book of Colossians

TODAY'S DATE: _____
DATE BOOK WAS WRITTEN _____

NAME OF LESSON _____
BIBLICAL TEXT _____

SCRIPTURE(S):
_____
_____
_____

Who wrote this book?
_____

What is Chapter 1 about?
_____
_____
_____
_____
_____
_____
_____
_____
_____
_____
_____
_____
_____
_____
_____

What is Chapter 2 about?
_____

What is Chapter 3 about?

What is Chapter 4 about?
_____
_____
_____
_____
_____
_____
_____
_____
_____
_____
_____
_____
_____
_____
_____

What are some key verses that stand out to you?
_____
_____
_____
_____
_____
_____
_____
_____

Any words from God?
_____

What revelation did you get from the text?

What is the entire book talking about?

POINTS FOR POWER: *(Write your points for Spiritual power through what the chapter is trying to convey that you will apply to your own life).*

1.

2.

3.

CHAPTER 13

The Book of 1 Thessalonians

TODAY'S DATE: _____
DATE BOOK WAS WRITTEN _____

NAME OF LESSON _____
BIBLICAL TEXT _____

SCRIPTURE(S):
_____
_____
_____

Who wrote this book?
_____

What is Chapter 1 about?
_____
_____
_____
_____
_____
_____
_____
_____
_____
_____
_____
_____
_____
_____

What is Chapter 2 about?
_____

What is Chapter 3 about?

What is Chapter 4 about?

What is Chapter 5 about?

What are some key verses that stand out to you?

Any words from God?

What revelation did you get from the text?

What is the entire book talking about?

POINTS FOR POWER: *(Write your points for Spiritual power through what the chapter is trying to convey that you will apply to your own life).*

1. _____
   _____
   _____
   _____

2.

3.

CHAPTER 14

The Book of 2 Thessalonians

The Biblical Bible Study Handbook

TODAY'S DATE: _____

DATE BOOK WAS WRITTEN _____

NAME OF LESSON _____

BIBLICAL TEXT _____

SCRIPTURE(S):
_____
_____
_____

Who wrote this book?
_____

What is Chapter 1 about?
_____
_____
_____
_____
_____
_____
_____
_____
_____
_____
_____
_____
_____
_____

What is Chapter 2 about?
_____

What is Chapter 3 about?

What are some key verses that stand out to you?
___

Any words from God?
___

What revelation did you get from the text?
___

What is the entire book talking about?

POINTS FOR POWER: *(Write your points for Spiritual power through what the chapter is trying to convey that you will apply to your own life).*

1. _____

2.

3.

CHAPTER 15

The Book of 1 Timothy

TODAY'S DATE: _____

DATE BOOK WAS WRITTEN _____

NAME OF LESSON _____

BIBLICAL TEXT _____

SCRIPTURE(S):

_____

_____

_____

Who wrote this book?

_____

What is Chapter 1 about?

_____
_____
_____
_____
_____
_____
_____
_____
_____
_____
_____
_____
_____
_____

What is Chapter 2 about?

_____

What is Chapter 3 about?

What is Chapter 4 about?

What is Chapter 5 about?

What is Chapter 6 about?

What are some key verses that stand out to you?

Any words from God?

What revelation did you get from the text?

What is the entire book talking about?

The Biblical Bible Study Handbook

POINTS FOR POWER: *(Write your points for Spiritual power through what the chapter is trying to convey that you will apply to your own life).*

1. _____

2.

3.

CHAPTER 16

The Book of 2 Timothy

TODAY'S DATE: _____

DATE BOOK WAS WRITTEN _____

NAME OF LESSON _____

BIBLICAL TEXT _____

SCRIPTURE(S):

_____

_____

_____

Who wrote this book?

_____

What is Chapter 1 about?

_____
_____
_____
_____
_____
_____
_____
_____
_____
_____
_____
_____
_____
_____
_____
_____

What is Chapter 2 about?

_____

What is Chapter 3 about?

What is Chapter 4 about?

What are some key verses that stand out to you?

Any words from God?

What revelation did you get from the text?

What is the entire book talking about?

POINTS FOR POWER: *(Write your points for Spiritual power through what the chapter is trying to convey that you will apply to your own life).*

1.

2.

3.

CHAPTER 17

The Book of Titus

TODAY'S DATE: _____
DATE BOOK WAS WRITTEN _____

NAME OF LESSON _____
BIBLICAL TEXT _____

SCRIPTURE(S):
_____
_____
_____

Who wrote this book?
_____

What is Chapter 1 about?
_____
_____
_____
_____
_____
_____
_____
_____
_____
_____
_____
_____
_____
_____
_____
_____

What is Chapter 2 about?
_____

What is Chapter 3 about?

What are some key verses that stand out to you?

Any words from God?

What revelation did you get from the text?

What is the entire book talking about?

POINTS FOR POWER: *(Write your points for Spiritual power through what the chapter is trying to convey that you will apply to your own life).*

1. _____

2.

3.

CHAPTER 18

The Book of Philemon

The Biblical Bible Study Handbook

TODAY'S DATE: _____
DATE BOOK WAS WRITTEN _____

NAME OF LESSON _____
BIBLICAL TEXT _____

SCRIPTURE(S):
_____
_____
_____

Who wrote this book?
_____

What is Chapter 1 about?
_____
_____
_____
_____
_____
_____
_____
_____
_____
_____
_____
_____
_____
_____

What are some key verses that stand out to you?
_____

Any words from God?

What revelation did you get from the text?

What is the entire book talking about?

POINTS FOR POWER: *(Write your points for Spiritual power through what the chapter is trying to convey that you will apply to your own life).*

1. _____

2.

3.

CHAPTER 19

The Book of Hebrews

TODAY'S DATE: _____
DATE BOOK WAS WRITTEN _____

NAME OF LESSON _____
BIBLICAL TEXT _____

SCRIPTURE(S):
_____
_____
_____

Who wrote this book?
_____

What is Chapter 1 about?
_____
_____
_____
_____
_____
_____
_____
_____
_____
_____
_____
_____
_____
_____

What is Chapter 2 about?
_____

What is Chapter 3 about?

What is Chapter 4 about?

What is Chapter 5 about?

What is Chapter 6 about?

What is Chapter 7 about?

What is Chapter 8 about?

What is Chapter 9 about?

What is Chapter 10 about?

What is Chapter 11 about?

What is Chapter 12 about?

What is Chapter 13 about?

What are some key verses that stand out to you?

Any words from God?

What revelation did you get from the text?

What is the entire book talking about?

POINTS FOR POWER: *(Write your points for Spiritual power through what the chapter is trying to convey that you will apply to your own life).*

1. _____

2. _____

3.

CHAPTER 20

The Book of James

TODAY'S DATE: _____
DATE BOOK WAS WRITTEN _____

NAME OF LESSON _____
BIBLICAL TEXT _____

SCRIPTURE(S):
_____
_____
_____

Who wrote this book?
_____

What is Chapter 1 about?
_____
_____
_____
_____
_____
_____
_____
_____
_____
_____
_____
_____
_____
_____
_____
_____

What is Chapter 2 about?
_____

What is Chapter 3 about?

What is Chapter 4 about?

What is Chapter 5 about?

What are some key verses that stand out to you?

Any words from God?

What revelation did you get from the text?

What is the entire book talking about?

POINTS FOR POWER: *(Write your points for Spiritual power through what the chapter is trying to convey that you will apply to your own life).*

1. _____
_____
_____
_____

2.

3.

CHAPTER 21

The Book of 1 Peter

TODAY'S DATE: _____
DATE BOOK WAS WRITTEN _____

NAME OF LESSON _____
BIBLICAL TEXT _____

SCRIPTURE(S):
_____
_____
_____

Who wrote this book?
_____

What is Chapter 1 about?
_____
_____
_____
_____
_____
_____
_____
_____
_____
_____
_____
_____
_____
_____
_____

What is Chapter 2 about?
_____

What is Chapter 3 about?

What is Chapter 4 about?

What is Chapter 5 about?

What are some key verses that stand out to you?

Any words from God?

What revelation did you get from the text?

What is the entire book talking about?

The Biblical Bible Study Handbook

POINTS FOR POWER: *(Write your points for Spiritual power through what the chapter is trying to convey that you will apply to your own life).*

1. _____
_____
_____
_____

2.

3.

CHAPTER 22

The Book of 2 Peter

TODAY'S DATE: _____
DATE BOOK WAS WRITTEN _____

NAME OF LESSON _____
BIBLICAL TEXT _____

SCRIPTURE(S):
_____
_____
_____

Who wrote this book?
_____

What is Chapter 1 about?
_____
_____
_____
_____
_____
_____
_____
_____
_____
_____
_____
_____
_____
_____
_____

What is Chapter 2 about?
_____

What is Chapter 3 about?

What are some key verses that stand out to you?
_____
_____
_____
_____
_____
_____
_____
_____
_____
_____
_____

Any words from God?
_____
_____
_____
_____
_____
_____
_____
_____
_____
_____
_____
_____

What revelation did you get from the text?
_____
_____
_____

What is the entire book talking about?

POINTS FOR POWER: *(Write your points for Spiritual power through what the chapter is trying to convey that you will apply to your own life).*

1. _____

2.

3.

CHAPTER 23

The Book of 1 John

The Biblical Bible Study Handbook

TODAY'S DATE: _____

DATE BOOK WAS WRITTEN _____

NAME OF LESSON _____

BIBLICAL TEXT _____

SCRIPTURE(S):

_____

_____

_____

Who wrote this book?

_____

What is Chapter 1 about?

_____
_____
_____
_____
_____
_____
_____
_____
_____
_____
_____
_____
_____
_____
_____

What is Chapter 2 about?

_____

What is Chapter 3 about?

What is Chapter 4 about?

What is Chapter 5 about?

What are some key verses that stand out to you?

Any words from God?

What revelation did you get from the text?

What is the entire book talking about?

_____
_____
_____
_____
_____
_____
_____
_____
_____
_____
_____
_____
_____
_____
_____
_____
_____
_____
_____
_____
_____
_____
_____
_____
_____
_____
_____
_____
_____
_____

POINTS FOR POWER: *(Write your points for Spiritual power through what the chapter is trying to convey that you will apply to your own life).*

1. _____
_____

2.

3.

CHAPTER 24

The Book of 2 John

TODAY'S DATE: _____

DATE BOOK WAS WRITTEN _____

NAME OF LESSON _____

BIBLICAL TEXT _____

SCRIPTURE(S):
_____
_____
_____

Who wrote this book?
_____

What is Chapter 1 about?
_____
_____
_____
_____
_____
_____
_____
_____
_____
_____
_____
_____
_____
_____
_____
_____

What are some key verses that stand out to you?
_____

Any words from God?

What revelation did you get from the text?

What is the entire book talking about?

POINTS FOR POWER: *(Write your points for Spiritual power through what the chapter is trying to convey that you will apply to your own life).*

1. _____

2.

3.

CHAPTER 25

The Book of 3 John

TODAY'S DATE: _____
DATE BOOK WAS WRITTEN _____

NAME OF LESSON _____
BIBLICAL TEXT _____

SCRIPTURE(S):
_____
_____
_____

Who wrote this book?
_____

What is Chapter 1 about?
_____
_____
_____
_____
_____
_____
_____
_____
_____
_____
_____
_____
_____
_____
_____

What are some key verses that stand out to you?
_____

Any words from God?

What revelation did you get from the text?

What is the entire book talking about?

POINTS FOR POWER: *(Write your points for Spiritual power through what the chapter is trying to convey that you will apply to your own life).*

1. _____

2.

3.

CHAPTER 26

The Book of Jude

TODAY'S DATE: _____

DATE BOOK WAS WRITTEN _____

NAME OF LESSON _____

BIBLICAL TEXT _____

SCRIPTURE(S):

_____
_____
_____

Who wrote this book?

_____

What is Chapter 1 about?

_____
_____
_____
_____
_____
_____
_____
_____
_____
_____
_____
_____
_____
_____
_____
_____

What are some key verses that stand out to you?

_____

Any words from God?

What revelation did you get from the text?

What is the entire book talking about?

POINTS FOR POWER: *(Write your points for Spiritual power through what the chapter is trying to convey that you will apply to your own life).*

1. _____

2.

3.

CHAPTER 27

The Book of Revelation

TODAY'S DATE: _____

DATE BOOK WAS WRITTEN _____

NAME OF LESSON _____

BIBLICAL TEXT _____

SCRIPTURE(S):

_____
_____
_____

Who wrote this book?

_____

What is Chapter 1 about?

_____
_____
_____
_____
_____
_____
_____
_____
_____
_____
_____
_____
_____
_____
_____

What is Chapter 2 about?

_____

What is Chapter 3 about?

What is Chapter 4 about?

What is Chapter 5 about?

What is Chapter 6 about?

What is Chapter 7 about?

What is Chapter 8 about?

What is Chapter 9 about?

What is Chapter 10 about?

What is Chapter 11 about?

What is Chapter 12 about?

What is Chapter 13 about?

What is Chapter 14 about?

What is Chapter 15 about?

What is Chapter 16 about?

What is Chapter 17 about?

What is Chapter 18 about?

What is Chapter 19 about?

What is Chapter 20 about?

What is Chapter 21 about?

What is Chapter 22 about?

What are some key verses that stand out to you?

Any words from God?

What revelation did you get from the text?

What is the entire book talking about?

POINTS FOR POWER: *(Write your points for Spiritual power through what the chapter is trying to convey that you will apply to your own life).*

1.

2.

3.

CONTACT STEPHANIE

For more information on Stephanie:

>info@stephaniefranklin.org
>www.stephaniefranklin.org

Stephanie Franklin, M.A. (T.H. /MDIV.)

Obtains two Master of Arts degrees in Theological Studies and a Master of Divinity, and has a vision to reach the world. She has a heart to reach the youth and young adults along with the entire family, bringing them all together as a unified fold. One of her greatest desires is to be used by God in whatever capacity He chooses.

www.ingramcontent.com/pod-product-compliance
Lightning Source LLC
Chambersburg PA
CBHW080725300426
44114CB00019B/2490